Where Babies Come From

**Stories to Help Parents Answer
Preschoolers' Questions About Sex**

By Martin Silverman, M.D., and Harriet Ziefert
Illustrated by Claire Schumacher

Random House 🏠 New York

Library of Congress Cataloging-in-Publication Data:
Silverman, Martin (Martin A.). Where babies come from.
SUMMARY: Animal stories illustrate the steps in reproduction from intercourse to the birth of a child. A separate section
gives sample answers parents may give to their children's questions.   ISBN: 0-394-82716-3 (trade); 0-394-92716-8 (lib. bdg.)
1. Sex instruction for children. [1. Reproduction. 2. Sex instruction for children] I. Ziefert, Harriet.
II. Schumacher, Claire, ill. III. Title.   HQ53.Z54 1989 612.6'007 89-8386

Manufactured in the United States of America   1 2 3 4 5 6 7 8 9 0

Introduction

This book is for parents to use to help their preschool children understand the complicated issues of sex and childbirth. From a very early age children are curious about sex and ask many questions, especially when a new baby is about to arrive. They need help from the start if they are to develop an accurate understanding and healthy attitudes by the time they reach adolescence.

Attitudes evolve slowly, and children are impressionable throughout their growing years. It is impossible to shield them from outside influences. Other children talk to them; they watch television; they see for themselves. All these influences can be complex and confusing.

Devoted parents are in the best position to guide their children's learning about sex, but they often find the task embarrassing. The four Little Elephant stories in this book are designed to help parents negotiate an otherwise difficult topic.

The stories not only furnish the information young children need; they also help children put their feelings about sexual matters into words, thereby making them more manageable. Our experiences, as a physician and an educator of young children respectively, show that children deal with complex, emotionally charged subjects more easily when they are presented indirectly. By using animal characters instead of humans, we help children maintain the emotional distance that is necessary for gaining understanding.

We suggest reading the stories to your child one at a time—perhaps a story a night for four nights. It is likely that your child will ask questions. To help you answer them, there is a list of typical questions and suggested answers at the back of the book.

Don't be worried if your child does not absorb or retain all the information at first. Children commonly distort the facts or elaborate their own fantasies. This is quite normal. If you are truthful and consistent, they will eventually get things clear.

We hope this book will be enjoyable as well as useful. We dedicate it to our children and to the children we have learned from in our work.

Martin Silverman, M.D., and Harriet Ziefert, M.A.

Whose Big Egg?

"Look what I found!" said Little Elephant to his friend Kikki. He showed the monkey a big egg, which he carefully cradled in his trunk.

Kikki looked at the big egg and said, "My mother told me babies grow inside eggs. But I don't know whose baby is inside this one. Do you?"

"No," answered Little Elephant. "Let's find out."

Little Elephant, with Kikki on his back, ran up to a giraffe. They both started talking at once.

"Is this your egg?" Little Elephant asked.

"Is your baby inside it?" asked Kikki.

"No, it's not my egg," answered the giraffe. "I do not lay eggs. When I have a baby, it grows inside my body."

Next they met a mother lion and her four cubs. Little Elephant asked, "Is this your egg?"

"No, it's not my egg," answered the mother lion. "I do not lay eggs. My cubs grew inside my body before they were born."

Little Elephant and Kikki came to a big water hole. There they spotted a mother antelope, a mother zebra, and a mother baboon.

Kikki asked each of them, "Is this your egg? Is this your egg? Is this your egg?"

"It's not mine!" said the antelope.

"It's not mine!" said the zebra.

"It's not mine!" said the baboon.

Mother Baboon splashed Little Elephant playfully and said, "We don't lay eggs. We carry our babies inside our bodies."

"So whose baby is inside this egg?" Little Elephant asked.

Mother Baboon laughed and said, "That egg is *so* big—maybe there's an elephant inside!"

Everyone except Little Elephant laughed at the joke. He didn't think it was funny. He turned and ran away.

He ran without stopping until he found his mother.

"I just ran all the way from the water hole," he said, trying to catch his breath. "No one there knew whose baby is inside this egg. And someone said the egg is big enough to be an elephant's!"

"Whoever said that must have been teasing you," said Mother Elephant.

"She was!" said Little Elephant. "I know elephants don't come from eggs! They come from mother elephants."

"You're right," said Mother Elephant. "You began as a tiny egg inside my body. You grew in my womb for a long time before you were born."

Little Elephant examined the egg carefully. He turned it around. He even held it to his ear. But he couldn't hear anything. Not one single sound.

Little Elephant kept quiet for a while. Then he spoke.

"Giraffes, lions, baboons, antelopes, zebras—and elephants— come from inside their mothers' bodies. So which babies come from outside their mothers' bodies?"

Mother Elephant answered, "Bird babies come from eggs outside their mothers' bodies. So do snakes and turtles and lizards."

"I don't think there's a snake or a turtle inside this egg," said Little Elephant. "I think there's a baby bird inside it."

"That's a good guess," said Mother Elephant.

"I *really* want to know which bird laid this egg!" he said.

"I think we can find out," answered his mother. "Let's go for a walk. We can look for eggs and nests."

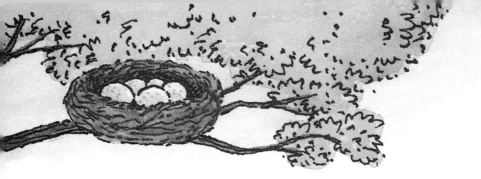

Little Elephant and his mother walked and walked. Nests were hard to spot. For a long time it seemed as if there were no nests anywhere.

Little Elephant found one first.

He pointed to a nest high up in a tree and said, "Look! Look! There are eggs in there. But I found my egg on the ground. And if it had fallen from a tree, it would have splattered with a great big splosh!"

Through an opening in the trees Little Elephant spotted an ostrich running through the grass.

"Let's follow him," suggested Mother Elephant. "I can tell by his size that he is a male. He might be bringing food to a mother ostrich who is sitting on a nest."

"Why doesn't the mother ostrich find her own food?" Little Elephant asked.

"Because she needs to stay with her eggs to keep them warm. And she needs to protect them from animals who might like to eat eggs."

They followed the ostrich through some thick bushes. While the big ostrich ran out into a clearing, Little Elephant and his mother waited behind some bushes. Through the leaves Little Elephant could see the mother ostrich standing beside her nest in the ground.

"Look! Look!" he said. "The eggs in that nest are just like the one I found! I'm going to give the mother ostrich the egg she lost."

"I don't think you should right now," answered Mother Elephant. "The ostrich mother is busy. And besides, you might scare her. I think something is going to happen. Why don't we just stay here and watch."

And that is just what they did until…

a baby ostrich was born!

Little Elephant Butts In

It was a warm morning in the grasslands. Little Elephant and Kikki were playing racing and chasing games. By midmorning it was hot. Very hot.

"I don't feel like playing anymore," said Little Elephant.

"Let's cool off at the water hole," said Kikki.

"Good idea," said Little Elephant. "I'd like to cover my whole self with water and nice, cool mud."

Little Elephant and Kikki went to the water hole.
Little Elephant took a bath.
Kikki splashed himself with water, then made funny faces at his reflection in the water. Silly monkey!

When they felt good and cool, they headed home.
Little Elephant and Kikki decided to take a shortcut through a clump of trees and shrubs. As they walked through the thicket, they stumbled onto something they had never seen before.

Two giraffes were standing close together. One was over the other one and was moving in a strange way.

Little Elephant and Kikki were surprised. They didn't know what to do. So they ran away.

Little Elephant stopped to catch his breath. Then he said, "Kikki, what was going on? What was the big giraffe doing?"

"I don't know," said Kikki. "It looked like he was trying to climb on top of her. But I'm not sure."

When Little Elephant got home, his mother asked, "Did you have fun with Kikki this morning?"

"Yes. We ran and played hide-and-seek," answered Little Elephant. "Then it got hot, so I took a bath."

"What else?"

"Nothing else—except we went into a thicket and saw two giraffes. One was on top of the other one. Can you tell me what they were doing?"

"Yes," said Little Elephant's mother. "I'll tell you."

Mother Elephant explained that the giraffes were doing something special that made them both feel good.

"But it looked like they were fighting!" said Little Elephant.

"They weren't fighting," said Mother Elephant. "They were making a baby."

"Making a baby!" exclaimed Little Elephant. "Are you sure?"

"Yes, I'm sure," said Mother Elephant.

Then Little Elephant remembered something his mother once said—that it took a mother and a father for a baby elephant to be born.

He asked, "What the giraffes were doing—is that what *elephants* do to make a baby?"

Mother Elephant flapped her ears the way elephants do to stay cool.

Then she answered Little Elephant's question.

"Giraffes and zebras and baboons and all the furry animals around here do the same thing to make a baby."

"Maybe zebras and giraffes and baboons do that," said Little Elephant. "But not elephants! And never *my* mother and father!"

Little Elephant ran away into some nearby bushes.

"Come back, my little elephant," his mother called.

She wanted to tell him that when a mother and a father elephant see how good it is to love each other, they want to have a little elephant they can *both* love together.

Suddenly Little Elephant charged out of the brush and butted headfirst into his mother's side.

"Ouch!" she cried out. "Why did you do that?"

"Because of what you said," answered Little Elephant. "And because I like to play games. And this is a game. It's called 'bump-in-the-belly.' "

Mother Elephant turned and said, "I've seen you play that game with your friends. But it's not a game to play with your mother. Some things you just can't do."

"But I want to!" said Little Elephant. "It's fun. Look! Birds play games too."

His mother looked up and saw two birds soaring and diving through the air.

The female landed on the branch of a tree. The male bird balanced himself on top of her and flapped his wings.

"I don't think they're playing," said Mother Elephant. "I think it's baby-making time for birds, too. It takes a mother and a father to make a baby bird. Soon Mother Bird will lay some eggs."

Little Elephant saw two antelopes running. He laughed and said, "Soon Mrs. Antelope will lay a great big egg!"

"You're playing a teasing game with me," said Mother Elephant. "You know antelopes don't lay eggs! Mrs. Antelope's baby will grow inside her body, the way you grew inside mine before you were born."

"Sometimes I like to tease," said Little Elephant.

Then he ran off again.

Soon Father Elephant returned. Mother Elephant was happy to see him. He nuzzled close and asked about her day.

Mother and Father Elephant were glad to have private time together. They stood next to each other and talked about the things grownups talk about when they are by themselves.

Suddenly a streak of gray flew out of the thicket. It thumped into the narrow space between the two big elephants.

Mother and Father Elephant looked down and were surprised to see a smiling little elephant snuggled between them.

"Where did *you* come from?" they asked.

Little Elephant smiled a big smile.

"I saw you snuggling," he said. "And I wanted to snuggle too!"

And so they did!

Boys and Girls—
What's the Difference?

The animals were glad when the rains came. The dry season was over. Soon the grass would spring up thick and green. There would be new leaves and tender young twigs on the trees. Once again there would be lots to eat.

Little Elephant and his friends liked the rain. It tickled their backs and necks and made the air smell fresh and clean.

But they were happy when the rain stopped. They could run and play again. It was fun to charge around among the bright-colored flowers in a game of tag.

The ground was wet and slippery.

As Little Elephant and his friends chased each other, they slipped and sloshed in the puddles and the squishy mud.

Little Elephant lost his footing. He fell *kerplop* into a large pool of water. He made such a big splash that everyone laughed.

Little Elephant saw lots of squiggly tadpoles swimming in the shallow water.

"Where did they come from?" he asked. "Did the rain wash them from the sky?"

"I don't think so," said Kikki. "I think tadpoles come from frogs."

"Are you sure?" Little Elephant asked. "What do frogs have to do with tadpoles?"

Kikki answered, "I don't know how it works—but tadpoles grow up to be frogs."

Tadpoles and frogs—something new!

Little Elephant ran home to tell his mother what he had learned.

"Mama, Mama, I have news for you!" he cried out. "I found a whole lot of baby tadpoles. The frogs make them in the water—the way I make mud pies."

"Who told you that?" asked his mother.

"I figured it out *all by myself*," said Little Elephant.

"You are clever!" replied Mother Elephant. "I'm proud of how smart you are. But there are some facts you should know about how babies are really made. It's time for you and your father to talk."

"How does my father know about tadpoles?" Little Elephant asked. "He's an elephant, not a frog!"

"Your father knows lots of things—not just about elephants!" Mother Elephant answered.

"I don't have to talk to anybody," said Little Elephant. "I already know all about babies. Mrs. Zebra is going to have one and I figured out how it happened all by myself. Mrs. Zebra went swimming. And Mr. Zebra got mad because she wasn't there. So he went looking for her."

Mother Elephant looked puzzled, so little Elephant continued.

"Mr. Zebra splashed into the water, all grumpy and grouchy, looking for Mrs. Zebra. He made such a commotion that the tadpoles swam in every direction to get away from him."

Little Elephant's mother was still puzzled.

"Mrs. Zebra ducked her head under the water," said Little Elephant. "When she opened her mouth, a tadpole swam in and she swallowed it. It went down into her stomach and grew into a baby. Soon she'll give birth to a big frog!"

Mother Elephant opened her eyes wide when she heard the end of Little Elephant's story. What an imagination!

"Did I give birth to a frog when you were born?" she asked.

Little Elephant answered, "You would have if you'd gone swimming after a rainstorm!"

At first Mother Elephant didn't know what to say.

Then she said, "Let's go find your father. I'd like him to hear your story."

They found Father Elephant at the water hole.

Father Elephant playfully sprayed Little Elephant with water.

"Stop!" said Little Elephant. "I've already had a bath today!"

Father Elephant stopped spraying.

Little Elephant told him his ideas about how babies are made.

Father Elephant liked Little Elephant's fantastic story.

But he could see he was a little mixed up.

"Mrs. Zebra did not swallow anything to become pregnant," Father Elephant said. "And her baby is not in her stomach. It is in her womb. For the baby zebra to begin, Mr. Zebra used his penis to put a sperm into Mrs. Zebra through her vagina. It combined with her egg and began to grow in her womb. The baby grew from Mrs. Zebra's egg and from Mr. Zebra's sperm."

"Where did the sperm come from?" asked Little Elephant.

"It came from Mr. Zebra's testicles. Each sperm is very, very tiny. A sperm looks something like a tadpole."

"Do I have sperm in my testicles?" asked Little Elephant.

"Not yet," said his father. "When you become an adult, your testicles will begin to make sperm."

Little Elephant had just one more question.

"Where did Mrs. Zebra's egg come from?"

"From her ovaries," answered Father Elephant. "When Mrs. Zebra grew up, little eggs began to come from her ovaries."

"I don't think that you should tell me any more," said Little Elephant. "Or I'll get mixed up all over again."

Little Elephant looked up at his father.

"Do you know everything?" he asked. "Do you know about birds? Look over there. Do you know which is the girl bird and which is the boy bird?"

Father Elephant looked up.

"Sometimes it's hard to tell," he said. "But I know those birds. The one with the long, black tail and the red-and-yellow feathers is male. The female has brownish feathers and a shorter tail."

"I learned so much today," said Little Elephant. "I have to find Kikki so I can tell him about it."

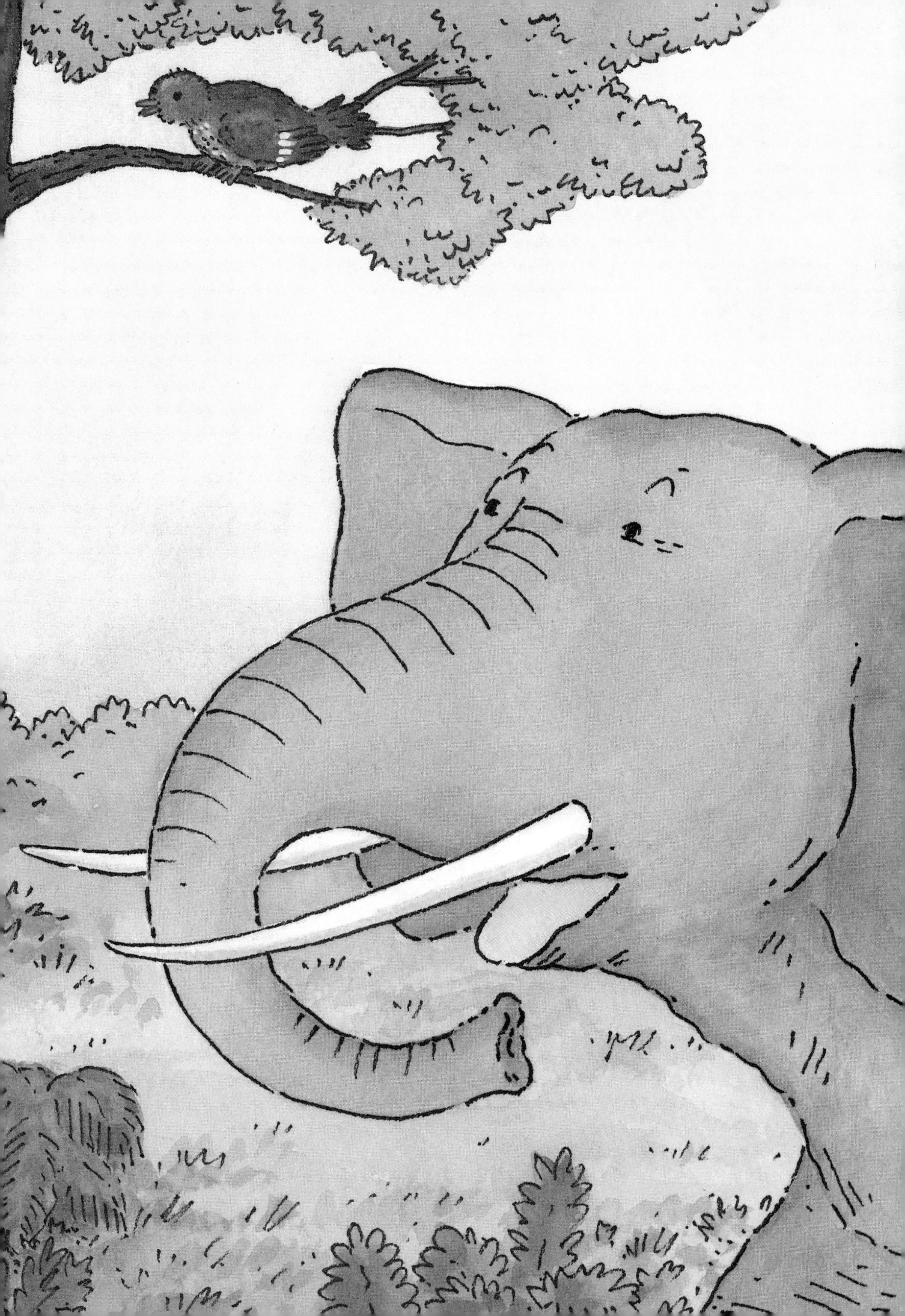

Little Elephant ran off to find Kikki. When he found him, he didn't stop talking for a long time.

A New Baby on the Way

Little Elephant was in the middle of a good game of hide-and-seek. He spotted a monkey tail poking out from behind a tree.

"Come out! Come out!" he shouted. "I see you."

Just then Little Elephant heard his mother call him.

"Oh no!" he said. "I have to go home, Kikki. But I see you behind that tree!" Then Little Elephant ran home.

"Why did you call me?" Little Elephant asked his mother. "I was in the middle of a game."

Mother Elephant answered, "I have something important I want to tell you before we visit Mrs. Giraffe."

"Okay," said Little Elephant. "But make it quick."

Mother Elephant told Little Elephant that she was pregnant. In a few months she would have a baby.

"Where is the baby?" asked Little Elephant. "Can I see it?"

"No," said Mother Elephant. "The baby is inside me—in my womb. You were there before you were born."

"Tell me again what I was like when I was first born," said Little Elephant. "I like hearing about it."

"You were small and cute," answered Mother Elephant. "When I looked at you and you looked back, I just wanted to hold you close and protect you."

Little Elephant said, "Mama, I like being your only little elephant. Why do you want a baby?"

Mother Elephant answered, "I like being a mother. I would like another little elephant just like you to love."

Little Elephant stamped his foot and said, "But one little elephant is enough!"

"I know you feel angry," said Mother Elephant. "But try to understand that if a mother has two elephants to love, her love grows, so there is twice as much, or more."

Little Elephant pushed against his mother's side. Before he was born, his mother's womb had kept him snug and warm. Now there was a new baby inside her. And that baby was making her look fat!

Little Elephant said, "I want to be inside you right now. Take the baby out so I can go back in."

Mother Elephant smiled. She said, "I understand your wish. But you can't have that wish, my little elephant."

Little Elephant looked sad.

Mother Elephant continued, "It's natural to feel jealous. But the baby inside me will not go away because of the way you feel. Besides, you've grown much too big to fit in my womb!"

Little Elephant was hungry. He pulled some leaves and bark from a tree and ate a big mouthful.

"I get bigger and bigger by eating lots of good food," he said to his mother. "What does the baby eat while it's inside you?"

"The baby gets everything it needs from a special tube called the umbilical cord," Mother Elephant answered. "The baby doesn't eat the way you do until after it is born."

"And what does the baby *do* inside you?" Little Elephant asked.

"The baby can move and kick—but not much else," answered Mother Elephant. "But the two of us—we can have fun together. Let's play a game."

"Can we play hide-and-seek?" asked Little Elephant.

Little Elephant and his mother started to play.
"I'll hide," said Little Elephant. "You be IT."
"Okay," said Mother Elephant. "You run and hide. I'll count to twenty."

"Come out! Come out, wherever you are!" called Mother Elephant when she finished counting. But there was no Little Elephant!

"Come out! Come out, wherever you are!" she called again.

Little Elephant's mother looked everywhere. But Little Elephant was nowhere to be found.

"Please, please, come out," Mother Elephant called. "I give up. I can't find you."

"Here I am!" shouted Little Elephant. "Now you can see me!"

And he ran out from behind a big rock.

"Now it's time to go visiting," said Mother Elephant. "I want you to come with me to visit Mrs. Giraffe. She just had a baby. And I want you to see it."

The baby giraffe was nursing.

"That's just how you sucked milk from me," said Mother Elephant.

"But not anymore!" said Little Elephant.

"Right!" said Mother Elephant. "Now you're big enough to eat leaves from trees. The baby giraffe will suck its mother's milk until it's big enough to eat leaves, too."

"Is the baby a boy or a girl?" Little Elephant asked.

"It's a boy," said Mother Giraffe.

Little Elephant turned to his own mother and said, "I want a baby brother, like him."

"We won't know until the baby is born," Mother Elephant said.

"Does my father know whether the baby is a boy or a girl?"

"No one knows," said Mother Elephant.

"Can we go home now?" Little Elephant asked.

"Yes," answered Mother Elephant. "Mother Giraffe and her baby have had enough company."

They found Father Elephant.

"I'm glad you're home," he said.

"And I'm glad I'm going to have a baby brother," said Little Elephant.

"Or a baby sister," added Mother Elephant.

"A baby sister!" cried Little Elephant. "I want a baby brother!"

"You can't have that wish," said Father Elephant. "You can't choose whether it will be a boy or a girl. Whatever it is, we're not going to give it back."

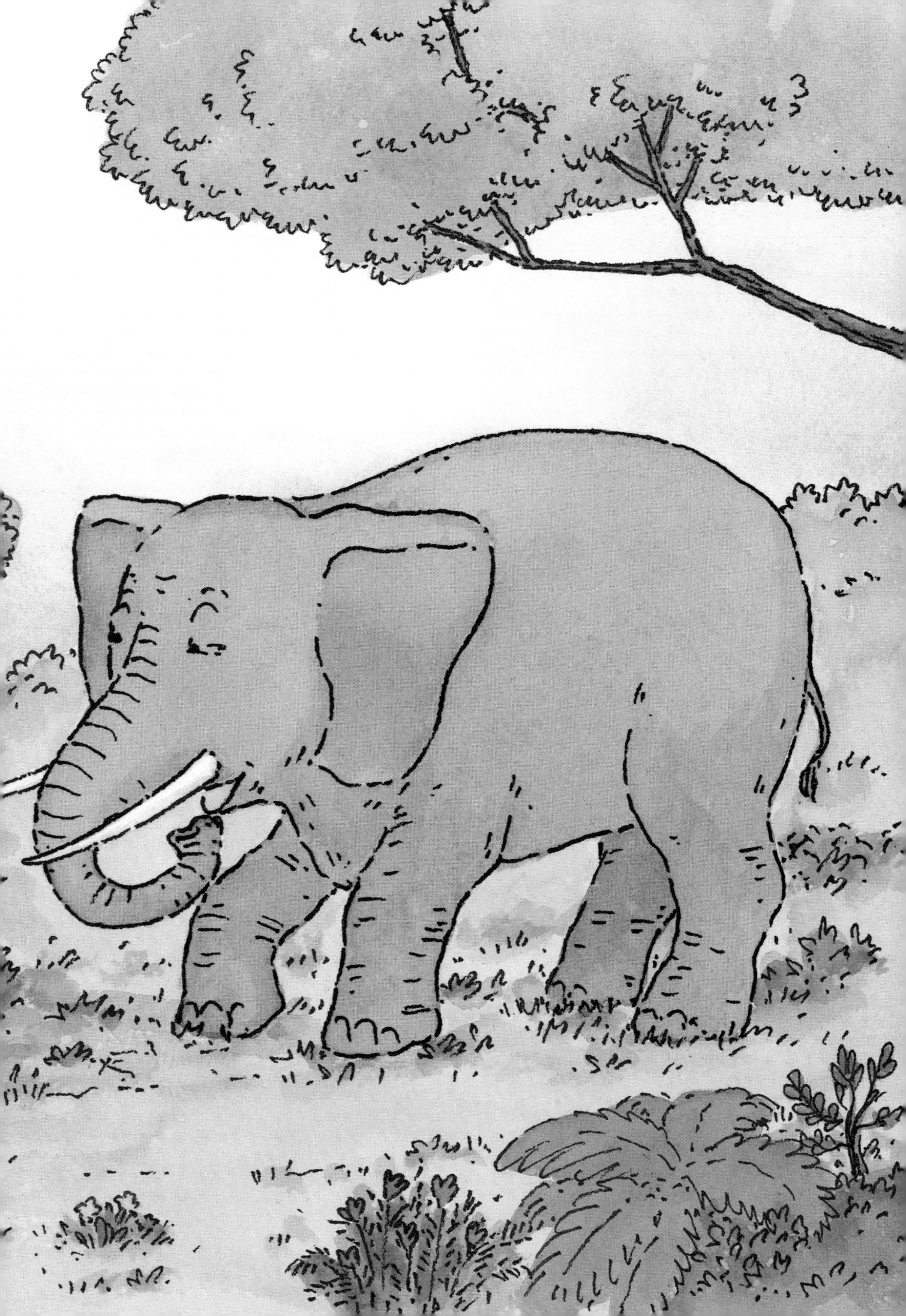

It was not very long before the new baby elephant was born. The Elephant family was all excited.

"Is it a boy or a girl?" Little Elephant asked immediately.

"It's a girl!" said Father and Mother Elephant proudly.

"And I'm her big brother!" said Little Elephant with a smile.

Questions Children Ask
and Answers Parents Might Give

Questions Children Ask About Pregnancy

"Mommy, where did I come from?"

Daddy and Mommy wanted a baby to love. Mommy had a tiny egg inside her, and Daddy put a teeny little sperm into Mommy's body. The sperm and the egg combined and grew into a baby. That baby was you.

"How did Daddy put the sperm into Mommy?"

Daddy and Mommy lay down close to each other so that Daddy could put the sperm into Mommy with his penis. The sperm came out of Daddy's penis and went into Mommy's vagina. It swam like a tadpole through Mommy's vagina until it got to the place where the egg was.

"Does it hurt when Daddy puts his sperm into Mommy's vagina?"

No, it feels good. They love each other and want to have a child. Mommy and Daddy enjoy making a baby together.

"Does the daddy make peepee into the mommy when they're making a baby?"

No. Sperm and urine never come out of the penis at the same time.

"Mommy, did I grow in your tummy?"

No, you grew in a special place called a womb. It's below Mommy's stomach. It stretched and got bigger and bigger as you got bigger.

"What did I eat when I was a baby inside you?"

Mommy fed you through a special tube that went from Mommy's body to your body. Feel where your bellybutton is. That's where the tube was attached to you. Everything you needed came through that tube. You didn't have to eat through your mouth until you were born.

"How did I get out from inside you?"

You came out through Mommy's vagina. It stretched so there would be enough room for you to come out.

"How did I know when to come out?"

You stayed in Mommy's womb for nine months. You grew bigger and bigger until there was no more room. It was time for you to be born. So Mommy's womb began working to push you out.

"Mommy, are there more babies inside you?"

No, but Mommy has more eggs in her ovaries. The ovaries let an egg out once a month. A mommy and daddy have to put a sperm and an egg together every time they want to have a baby.

"Are there babies inside Daddy?"

No. Daddies can't have babies, but without sperm there would be no babies. Daddy's testicles produce sperm all the time. For a baby to be made, the daddy's sperm is just as important as the mommy's egg.

Questions Girls Ask About Their Bodies

"Mommy, am I going to have breasts like you?"

You will have breasts when you are older, and you'll grow hair on certain parts of your body too, just like Mommy. Women and girls both have nipples, but little girls have to wait until they grow up before they develop breasts.

"What's inside my vagina?"

Your vagina goes from the outside of your body to the inside of your body. On the inside are your ovaries and your womb. When you grow up, your ovaries will let an egg out every month so you'll be able to have a baby. And your womb will become big enough for a baby to grow inside it. But to have a baby, you'll have to wait until you are old enough to be responsible for it.

"Is there a penis inside my vagina?"

There is no penis inside your vagina. You were born with everything a girl needs to have. You don't need a penis and you won't grow one.

"Does peepee come from my vagina?"

No, it comes out through a separate opening just above your vagina. And above the opening for the peepee is a special part of the girl's body called a clitoris. Your vagina and your clitoris are covered by folds to protect them.

"Mommy, can I see your vagina? Can I see Daddy's penis?"

Some things are private between grownups and children. Grownups don't show their vaginas and penises to children. And, except for going to the doctor for a checkup, children don't show theirs to grownups who might ask to see them. But you can look with a mirror to see how you are made.

Questions Boys Ask About Their Bodies

"What's a bellybutton for?"

While you were still inside the womb, you were fed through a special tube called an umbilical cord. It went from inside Mommy's body to your body, where your bellybutton is now. Everybody has a bellybutton.

"What's under my penis?"

Your testicles are under your penis. When you grow up and become a man, they will begin to produce sperm. Then you'll be able to become a daddy, because it takes a sperm and an egg to make a baby. The man's sperm is just as important as the woman's egg.

"Why does my penis get bigger sometimes?"

Sometimes your penis gets bigger because you have to urinate. But sometimes your penis gets bigger all by itself. It's one step in your body's preparation for the time when you're a grown-up man and ready to become a daddy.

"When will my penis be as big as Daddy's?"

As you grow bigger your penis and testicles will get bigger, like Daddy's. You'll grow more hair on your body, and you'll shave your face, like Daddy does.

"Can I have a baby?"

Boys and men don't have a vagina and ovaries and a womb. They don't give birth to babies. Only a grown-up woman can have a baby. But when you become a man, your testicles will begin to produce sperm, and you'll be able to become a daddy. But to be a father, you'll have to wait until you are old enough to be responsible for a baby.

"Do girls have penises inside them?"

No. Girls never have a penis. They're made differently from boys from the time they're born. Girls have a vagina and there's no penis inside it.

"Can I lose my penis?"

You can never lose your penis. Boys are born with a penis and testicles and they always stay that way. No one will ever take them away.

"Will I get breasts?"

No. All boys and girls and men have nipples. But only grown-up women have breasts. When a woman gives birth, her breasts produce milk for the baby. Girls get breasts when they grow up into women. Boys grow up into men, so they don't grow breasts.

"Daddy, can I see your penis? Can I see Mommy's vagina?"

Some things are private between grownups and children. Grownups don't show their vaginas and penises to children. And, except for going to the doctor for a checkup, children don't show theirs to grownups who might ask to see them. But you can look at yourself in the mirror to see how you are made.